MW00930513

HOW TO BECOME A SUCCESSFUL FREIGHT BROKER
Easy to Follow Step by Step Training Guide

By George A. Stewart

Copyright © 2013 - CSB Academy Publishing Co.

A personal Thank you from me for
trying my book, I would love to hear
your feedback on Amazon.
To show my appreciation, I have decided
to offer everyone that buys my book a
free copy of all future update of this
book.
Just register your name at:
www.FreightBrokerTrainingGuide.com

TABLE OF CONTENTS

INTRODUCTION

MY NAME IS GEORGE A. STEWART, I am 43 years old, I worked 12 years as a store manager for Burger King Restaurant, a truly dead end job. Just like most jobs in the market today I used to put in plenty of hours that unfortunately, did not translate into money. I understand that everyone has bad days at work; for me it was not an ordinary occasional dissatisfaction but a genuine mismatch. Working for long hours and under constant stress was taking a toll on my health and to make matters worse I was earning $36,500 per year, which was barely enough to feed myself, my wife and three children. Most of the time, I felt like I was dangling from a cliff.

My turning point was the day I met a certain customer in my restaurant who seemed to be doing very well despite the hard economic times the whole country was going through. After a little chitchat, I found out he was a freight broker and that he was earning a decent living while working a few hours.

At that point I did not know anything about freight brokerage or that a profession like that even existed. I therefore decided to do some research about it and the more I learnt, the more my interest grew and within a matter of weeks I was completely hooked up. Before I knew it, I took time off work to begin my training in freight brokerage.

After my training, I decided to quit my job at burger king and took up a job as a freight agent working under an established freight broker. My job included looking for new clients, taking orders and matching shippers with carriers. In one year or so I felt that I had enough experience and contacts to start my own firm. I then applied for the required licenses at FMCSA and started small.

Starting my own firm was definitely not easy but I found it much better than working at burger king. My first client was a contact I had made from working as a freight agent. After a lot of hard work I finally started getting more clients, and in 6 months I could finally relax because my business had finally taken off. I was earning around $120,000 every year, which, I must confess, was really good for starters. Now that I can work for fewer hours per day, my stress level has gone down and health wise, I am on the road to recovery. I can take better care of my family and also spend a lot more time with them.

After reading this book, if you get the interest in learning more about this business, you can also visit my blog at *http://freightbrokertrainingguide. com/*.

Why I wrote this book

My success as a freight broker has made me feel like I owe other people who are working hard like I did for many years. A few years ago I did not have any idea about freight brokerage and the freight business. Today this business has changed my life and I would like to make a difference in your life. I am forever grateful to that customer at Burger King who told me about freight brokerage. In my career as a freight broker I have gained a lot of experience and inside information that I would like to share with you. For me, if the information that is contained in this book helps even one person to change his or her life for the better then, I will consider this book a success.

THE OBJECTIVE OF THIS BOOK

Now **THAT YOU KNOW** my story, and how I became a freight broker without a college degree, I believe that you can too. My objectives of writing this book are:

- To explain what freight brokering really is.
- To help you understand the process of freight brokering from start to finish.
- To give you the tools you need to be a successful freight broker
- To help you learn the daily operations of a brokerage agency
- To teach you techniques such as negotiating, rating, prospecting, sales and marketing.
- To help you manage any shipment from its origin to its destination.
- To help you gain valuable industry resources.

This book will provide you with general information about freight brokers. This book includes detailed steps and processes that you require to actually set up and function as a freight broker.

From this book, you will learn what to expect as you get started and what you need in order to be properly organized. You will also gather particular vital requirements that are needed for you to maintain and grow your business.

DEFINITION OF A FREIGHT BROKER

THIS IS THE TEXTBOOK definition of a freight broker.

"A freight broker is a go-between who connects shippers to carriers. Freight brokers organize for the transportation of a shipment between shippers and motor carriers. They are logistics specialists in the trucking transportation industry."

Over the years, I have noted that even though broker agents work with various types of transportation, all of them essentially operate as the negotiator between a shipper with a consignment and a carrier irrespective of whether the carrier is an airline, a railway, a motor carrier or any other means of transport. Despite these different modes of transportation, this report will focus on agents working in the trucking industry.

Broker agents normally work for a freight broker as an independent contractor. The agent will be responsible for his or her own income and self- employment taxes. There is no employer/employee relationship so, normally; there are no employee benefits.

The broker agent is not required to obtain his or her broker authority because he or she will work under the authority, or umbrella, of the freight broker they contract with.

The broker agent is not responsible for invoicing customers or for paying motor carriers. The basic function will be to find new customers, take orders on loads that need to be moved and then find qualified trucks that are ready, willing and able to transport the cargo.

Essentially, the agent assumes a fiduciary responsibility and obligation to the freight broker. In other words, a broker agent needs to be honest, diligent and reliable.

In an industry that is so vast and varied a wide range of participants are required for it to flourish. Although some of the participants' titles may be a little unclear, and some of their duties may overlap, we will keep things as clear and simple as possible, by looking at who the key players are and what they do.

The objective of this book

OTHER DEFINITIONS

Shipper/ consigner

- A shipper is a person or business that deals with products or goods for transport. A shipper is person or company in the business of transporting cargo.
- The job of a shipper is to guarantee the delivery of the freight to their customer, whether internal or external, in the right condition, at the right time, at the right price, legally, and in the most efficient way that optimizes the supply chain that is balancing risk with costs the company is willing to bear.
- A shipper needs to equalize the risks related to transporting goods with the willingness to pay for the protection of the freight and consequences of any service failure, non-compliance with rules and regulations, or exposure to liabilities under contracts of carriage and related logistics services.

Motor carrier

- A motor carrier is a business that provides truck transportation. There are two types of motor carriers:
  - Private (a company that provides truck transportation of its own cargo) and
  - For hire (a company that is paid to provide truck transportation of cargo belonging to others).

Freight forwarder

- Often confused with freight brokers, freight forwarders are significantly different. Forwarders typically take possession of the goods, consolidate numerous smaller shipments into one large shipment, then arrange for transport of that larger shipment using various shipping methods, including land, air and water carriers.
- These are individuals who facilitate imports and exports. Import-export brokers interact with U.S. Customs, other government agencies, international carriers, and other companies and organizations that are involved in international freight transportation.

Agricultural truck broker

- They are generally small and operating in a single of the country, unregulated agricultural truck brokers organize motor carrier service intended exempt agricultural products.

Shipper's associations

- Shipper's associations are generally exempt, charitable, cooperative corporations formed by of shippers to reduce transport prices by means of pooling consignments. Shipper's associations function in a manner much like that of freight forwarders, but their service is limited to members only.

HOW THE INDUSTRY WORKS

- I will begin by breaking down the industry. First there has to be freight that needs to be transported somewhere by someone. Whether it is a load of potatoes or a pallet of newspapers, it all has to be taken somewhere. Freight is not just described as commodities that are delivered on a motor carrier. It also involves airfreight, container freight, and rail, among others.
- Freight can be manufactured either locally or overseas. It is then shipped in to other parts of the world and needs to be delivered. Whether it is ports or factory loading docks, it is loaded on to a piece of equipment for transportation. This could be a truck, train, boat or even an airplane.
- All of this freight is handled through several parties. When a load of freight is manufactured it is intended for a certain customer. This could be a box of utensils heading to a retailer or a load of grains headed for a silo. Either way, there is always a shipper and a receiver. Sometimes, the freight goes through a third party that is a freight forwarder or freight broker.
- A freight broker acts as a middleman who handles the booking of the trucking company or any other mode of transport for the shipper. The broker usually approaches a shipper asking to help them handle their freight. This takes some burden off of a manufacturers shipping division. The shipper and broker negotiate an amount for each load, and the broker in turn hires a trucking company at a lower rate to help in delivering the shipment.

- A freight forwarder is identical to an agent but handles more global shipments. They will handle freight such as, container ship freight, air cargo going overseas, among others. For example, a car broker selling a car to someone overseas. The car broker will contact freight forwarders to quote a rate to ship the boat overseas.

- There are also 3PL companies. They handle all phases of hauling. They handle everything a broker and freight forwarder should handle, and more. Warehousing, rail, container, cold storage, and airfreight are all sides a 3PL will handle. They are generally very big companies with many departments.

- In some settings, a broker and freight forwarder work together. A broker will handle cargo that needs to go overseas and will need to seek the services of freight forwarder. However this is not similar to when a broker works with another broker. That is called double brokering. It is frowned upon in the industry, but it still happens. Double brokering can cause serious liability issues that are not needed.

- Trucking companies are unlikely to support a broker because they feel a broker takes advantage of them by taking money out of their pockets. In anyway, they do. Although most trucking companies dislike brokers, they need them. Brokers manage a large quantity of the freight that it is crucial for a broker to be used on occasion. Trucking companies have dispatchers and load planners that are accountable for booking freight for the trucks. They will usually call their own customers first, and use brokered freight as a last choice. From my experience, trucking companies that haul a lot of brokered freight are more likely to experience financial trouble. A trucking company requires a resilient book of business of their own. I find that smaller trucking companies tend to overlook the sales side and trust brokers. This can quickly spell trouble. If I could recommend one thing to any trucking company it would be to employ a good sales agent.

- As for brokers, they have their large companies that own large portions of freight that they can propose low rates to gain more freight. Since they own large portions of the market, they can undertake lower rates from customers and in turn be assured to sell it to a trucking company. The trucking companies have to take this cheap freight on occasionally because the brokerage handles a lot of freight. These brokerages are usually disliked in the industry. They are seen as rip off trucking companies because of their attitude in the market and their market share.

- There are also large trucking companies that function the same way as the large brokers. These trucking companies can underbid the smaller brokers and smaller trucking companies. They can do this because of the quantity of the market they can control. They generally get great rates from a client close to their domestic terminal and can manage to take less rates on their backhaul. This causes extremely low rates in the market that smaller companies cannot afford to accept. The other aspects are that these large companies have paid for equipment and have less operating costs and therefore bigger profit margins.

THE LIFE CYCLE OF A LOAD

- A load can be described as product that a shipper needs to move to a consignee. The shipper is also referred to as a client. The consignee is the person who receives the freight.
- Once you get the business of a client, they will start to offer certain loads. When you accept these loads, you have to sell the load to a carrier at a lower rate than you offered the client. Once you decide to cover the load for this client, you begin to search for a truck that wants the load. You then discuss a rate with that trucking company. Once you have agreed on the terms, you will set that carrier up. They will send you their set up packet. It usually contains their MC # (authority), their insurance, W9, and references. In turn you will send them your set up packet that usually contains the same information. After they have faxed back the signed broker/carrier contract; this is a contract stating that they will not go back to solicit your client for freight, do you go any further. You never give out any detailed information on who your client is until they have signed the contract. Once they have done that, you then fax them a rate confirmation so that they sign it and fax it back. You now have that load covered.
- A load starts as a product that is manufactured at a factory or plant. It is then selected for delivery to a buyer of those commodities. The load is then either organized for shipment by the shipping department or is handled by a third party. The load is vended to a carrier of the product by the shipping department or third party/broker. The carrier is

then accountable for delivering the load to a consignee. The consignee can be a buyer, retail store, another factory for further processing, or warehouse.

- The load can also be handled on other terms such as a load of cars being transported to another dealer or a load that was conveyed prior to a warehouse. There are many origins and destination combinations that can be had in this business. Products we use every day are put through this cycle for us to obtain them. Think of all of the important items in your home. They are there because of this industry and this cycle.

ROLE OF A FREIGHT BROKER

A FREIGHT BROKER IS A third party individual responsible for matching the load with the carrier from the shipper to the consignee. Freight brokers are in business because they take a huge load off the manufactures' shipping department by managing their shipments. The broker is responsible for quoting a rate to the shipper for the load, finding a carrier, negotiating a rate with the carrier and ensuring that the load is delivered. While doing this a freight broker should make a decent profit between the rates that they charge the client and the rate they pay the carrier.

- They are specialists in the tracking industry. Logistics is the overall process of manufacturing, holding, transporting and distributing goods in the most efficient economic manner possible.
- Freight brokers play a contributing role in expediting the shipping process. When companies are ready to ship goods to another location, they may use their own drivers and trucking fleet to do the job. However, some companies cut costs by outsourcing the work. Such companies enlist the services of freight brokers to arrange for carriers to handle tasks of picking up, transporting and delivering the goods.
- Freight brokers own firms that offer freight brokerage services to companies on a contractual basis. Some of the brokers are solo practitioners while others employ freight agents, who may be independent contractors themselves.
- Freight brokers act as liaisons between their clients and carriers. These brokers don't deliver shipments nor do they

ever handle the items that their clients need to be shipped. Their sole job is to locate carriers that offer the best rates for delivering goods for clients within specified schedules.

- Freight brokers perform routine tasks with every job they receive. They talk with clients to determine their shipping needs, what items they are shipping, where they ship them, when the shipment need to reach their destination, how much clients are willing to pay for shipping among others. Brokers can then identify the most appropriate carriers and contact them.

- Brokers negotiate freight rates with carriers so that they can satisfy their clients, make a profit for themselves and make a profit for the carrier. After an agreement has been made it is up to the broker to do all the necessary paperwork brokers are also responsible for making appointments for the shipment to be picked up or delivered he/she can also request the carriers to perform this task on his/her behalf. They monitor the delivery of cargo and bill the client once the job has been completed there after pay carriers for their transportation services.

- Since freight brokers are business owners, they are responsible of for performing various duties to ensure the success of their business. For example establishing client fees, developing standard contracts, maintaining proper insurances and licenses paying for taxes, bills and carrier fees. They also set aside time to look for new clients and more resource contacts in the trucking industry.

REQUIREMENTS OF BEING A FREIGHT BROKER

- I would recommend to anyone who would like to be freight broker he/she should start by working in the freight industry before starting his or her own brokerage. Here you will not only gain technical expertise but you will also make contacts that are important to the success of the business. To develop a wider scope of operations, some brokers may decide to use agents. Freight agents are independent contractors who work in a specific area. By starting out as a freight agent you will first of all gain the experience you need and also get important contacts that will assist you once you start your own office.
- For this reason, starting out as a freight agent rather than a broker will be more   reasonable. A freight agent's job is related to what a broker does, but the agent works under the guidance of the broker and the broker is the one responsible for issues such as paying carriers and sustaining the necessary surety bond.

USDOT Number

- Before starting a freight brokerage business you should first apply for a USDOT number (U.S. Department of Transportation number) with the Department of Transportation. The USDOT number is a unique identifier used in collecting and monitoring the safety information of a company that is acquired during inspections crash investigations audits and compliance reviews. Although it is not particularly required for someone who wants to become a freight broker, the USDOT number is necessary when filling out the application to become a broker through the FMCSA (Federal Motor Carrier Safety Administration).

Broker Authority

- This is a license that is provided by the FMCSA permitting persons or companies to act as freight brokers. Broker authority is applied for by filling out FMCSA form OP-1 and choosing the "broker of property" option. To fill in form OP-1 you will require individual or company contact information, the company name filed on a doing business as form (if applicable), and the applicant's USDOT number. A $300 fee is required for the application.

Surety Bond or Trust Fund

- It acts as insurance, which guarantees that the shipping corporations will be remunerated for their cargo space. If the shipper does not pay for the shipping service, the cost is absorbed by the freight brokerage; if they will not be able to pay, the bond company or trust fund will cover the expense. A freight broker must have a surety bond or trust fund worth $10,000 or more. A detailed credit and background check is usually needed before a surety bond is issued. Evidence of the surety bond or trust fund is filed with the FMCSA using form BMC-84 or BMC-85.

Legal Process Agent

- Freight brokerage businesses must register legal process agents with the FMCSA for each state they operate in. The job of the process agent is to provide legal representation within their state, though law firms with members in various states may be retained for use in each of these states. Process agents are registered with the FMCSA using form BOC-3, with spaces provided on the form for every state. A filing fee of $50 is required with form BOC-3.

The Application Process to Obtain Broker Authority

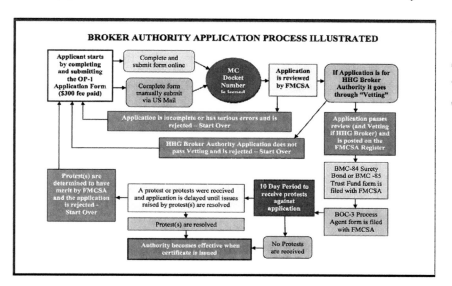

BROKER AUTHORITY APPLICATION PROCESS ILLUSTRATED

- Applications for operating authority are governed by rules that are stated in regulations, 49 CFR 365 and 366. When you want to obtain operating authority as a broker you should start by filling FMCSA's application for Motor Property Carrier and Broker Authority Form (OP-1). The OP-1 form can be downloaded as a Portable Document Format (PDF) file from FMCSA's Website at *http://www.fmcsa.dot.gov/forms/print/r-l-forms.htm.*
- You can also file the OP-1 application online. You can apply online at *http://www.fmcsa.dot.gov/online-registration.* This method is highly recommended. You can follow step-by-step instructions to assist you in completing the online OP-1 form for the appropriate broker authorities.
- After you download the OP-1 form you can input the required information directly on the form from your computer and then print it out. You can also print out a blank form and fill in the information manually. If you cannot access the FMCSA

Website, then you can request an OP-1 form packet be sent to you by U.S.Mail by contacting them at 1-800-832-5660.

- When you finish filling in the application, you may submit the form via U.S.Mail. The OP-1 form comes with instructions to assist you in completing and submitting the form. There is an initial application fee of $300.00 for each authority requested. The fee is non-refundable. If you file by U.S.Mail, then you may submit a check or money order, in U.S. dollars, payable to FMCSA to the address:

FMCSA
P.O. Box 530226,
Atlanta, GA 30353-0226.

If you choose to send it by Express U.S. Mail, then the address is

Bank of America,
Lockbox Number 530226,
1075 Loop Road,
Atlanta, GA 30337.

If you file online, then you submit payment using a credit or debit card.

- When filling in the application it is important to show proof of your financial responsibility. Financial Responsibility protects your business against liability. All brokers should have either a Surety Bond or a Trust Fund as proof of Financial Responsibility. Verification of financial responsibility is a necessary condition to obtaining and maintaining operating authority. Without it you cannot be granted authority as a broker. As a broker, you must submit a Property Brokers Surety Bond (Form BMC-84) as confirmation of a surety bond covering your business or a Property Brokers Trust Fund Agreement (Form BMC-85) as proof of a trust fund.
- Another important part of your application for broker authority is the Form BOC-3, Designation of Agent for Service of Process (often referred to as a process agent).
- A process agent is the person who will accept legal process on your behalf and forward it to you for response. Brokers are required to authorize a process agent for each State where they have offices or write contracts as stated in 49 CFR 366.4(b).

- For example, if your brokerage is located in Minnesota and you have offices in California and Arizona, you must designate process agents in all three states to be in compliance with the regulation.
- Additionally, if you have written agreements or contracts with motor carriers in Virginia and New York, then you must designate a process agent in those two states, too.
- The application process is then complete after you have filled OP-1 Form, BMC-84 or 85Form, and BOC-3 Form. Make sure you check the forms for accuracy before you submit them. Errors and omissions usually delay the processing of your application, eventually delaying the granting of your authority.

The FMCSA Review of Broker Applications

- After you submit your application for broker authority, FMCSA staff will review it. The Federal regulationat49CFR365.109 requires that FMCSA staff review your application for correctness, completeness, and adequacy of the evidence that you, as a broker, have the required amount of financial responsibility and are fit, willing, and able to comply with all applicable statutes and regulations.
- If minor errors are found on your application they may be corrected while going through the review process; nonetheless, incomplete applications will be rejected. It is crucial that, before you file your application, check the form and make sure that all the information is accurate, and that the form is complete.
- Follow the instructions that come with the OP-1 form, online closely. If you are applying for household goods a broker authority has to go through an additional step in the review process.
- In order to protect consumers from deceptive business practices in the industry, applicants for household goods broker authority undergo vetting. The information that is submitted by the applicant is closely examined, and in many cases verified to ensure that the applicant has not avoided responsibility for non-compliance with Federal regulations by using the name of another company. Vetting can be done for up-to 10 weeks. If you are applying for authority as a household goods broker,

you should make sure that your application is accurate, and avoiding any omissions on the application.

- If any omitted information is discovered during the application could be rejected. If the FMCSA review of your application finds it acceptable, then a notice of the application will be posted in the FMCSA Register. If you have not done so during the application process, you must submit a Form BMC-84, to show evidence that your brokerage is covered by a surety bond of $10,000 or $25,000, depending on type of brokerage, property or household goods. A Form BMC-85is the required evidence that your brokerage is covered by a trust fund of $10,000 or 25,000beforeauthority may be granted.

- Afterwards, a summary of your application for authority is posted in the FMCSA Register. Here any person who opposes the approval of your application on the grounds that you are not fit, willing, and able to comply with FMCSA's regulations has 10daysfrom the date of publication in the FMCSA Register to file a protest. If no one opposes the application, then a certificate will be issued making it effective.

An example of a freight broker license

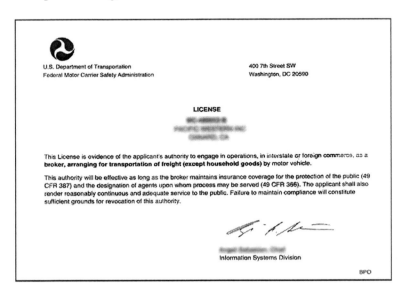

WRITING A BUSINESS PLAN

A **BUSINESS PLAN CAN BE** described as a written report about a plan of action. Business plans are born in the minds of entrepreneurs and are delivered in writing.

1. Executive Summary:

- It usually comes after the title page. It should clearly state what you exactly want without using too many words. It should be brief, precise and very formal.
- The executive summery should cover around half a page to one full page depending on how complex the funds will be used. In that space you should be able to give an outline of the entire business plan.

2. Market Analysis:

- Here you should show how much you know about the industry that your business is in. This section forces you to become familiar with all the aspects of the market that you are involved with enabling you to define the target market and position your company in a way that it will collect its share of sales.
- Market analysis will also help you to establish pricing, distribution and marketing strategies that will enable your company become profitable even in the most competitive markets. It will also show you the growth potential of the industry allowing you to make growth estimates for the future.

- You should begin your market analysis by defining the market according to size, its structure, growth prospects trends and sales potential.

3. *Company Description:*

- In this section you should describe how all the different elements of your business work together. It should include information about what your business deals with and also why you think your business will be a success

4. *Organization and Management:*

- This section should cover your company's organizational structure, aspects of the ownership of your company, accounts of your management team and testimonials of your panel of experts or board of directors.

5. *Marketing and Sales Strategies:*

- This is the most important aspect of your business. Marketing creates clients and the clients generate sales. In this section, you should define your marketing strategies.
- You should begin with strategies, tactics and channels that you normally use to be successful. Do not be afraid to note others that have worked for your competitors. This section will always be updated depending on your results.

6. *Service and/or Product Line:*

- This section should describe your services and products. You should describe exactly what it is that you are selling making sure that you emphasize on the benefits and not the features.
- You should create your own unique selling proposal. This will show how your product is different and also why it is better.

7. *Funding Requirements:*

- In this section you should state the amount of money you will require to start or expand your business. I will advise you to include best and worst case scenarios but be realistic.

8. *Financials:*

- This should be done after you have analyzed the market and you have set clear goals. This should include three to five years of historical data

Why you should write a business plan.

- A written business plan should give you focus and show whether the business is financially feasible.
- It will also show you what you need to continue the business, how much it is costing you to run your business and will help you get financing for your business.
- A good business plan will show you who your customers area, how competition can help you gain or lose customers and how you can acquire new customers.
- The business plan will show you the demographics of your business area, and the problems you are most likely going to run into.
- It should also show you what your employees should be doing, your strength and weakness and most of all it should be an inspiration to those who read it.

SETTING UP AN OFFICE

- In a freight brokerage business, you will be a middleman acting between individuals and businesses with freight to ship and carriers who are willing to handle their cargo. To be successful, you will need to form business relations with dependable, competent and trustworthy carriers and find ways to engage those in need of your services.
- The following table will show you an estimate of the necessary initial expenses for a freight brokerage. However this depends on whether you start as a home based business or if you want to get an office in a commercial location, and whether you hire employees right away or do everything yourself in the beginning. This operating capital should be enough to cover the first three months of operation and must be sufficient to cover what it will cost to pay the carriers before the shippers pay;
  - Rent: $0-$1,000
  - Equipment: $6,000-$22,000
  - Licenses/tax deposits: $200-$400
  - Advertising/marketing: $500-$1,500
  - Utilities/phone: $100-$300
  - Professional services: $200-$750
  - Payroll: $0-$5,000
  - Supplies: $300-$500
  - Insurance (first quarter): $700-$1,400
  - Suggested operating capital: $5,000-$250,000 (cash or line of credit)

Basic Office Equipment

Although may be tempting to fill up your office with a lot of clever gadgets that are designed to make your working life easier and fun, you are better off buying what you need at first. Consider these basic items:

- Typewriter - for filling out pre-printed and multipart forms
- Computer and printer
- Software - including accounting, customer information management and other administrative programs, and programs designed specifically for freight brokers
- Modem or any other means of internet connection
- Copy machine
- Fax machine
- Postage scale
- Postage meter
- Paper shredder
- Telecommunications equipment - including a telephone, voice mail, cell phone, pager, toll-free number and e-mail.

Location

- One of the most interesting aspects of a freight brokerage business is that your physical startup needs are rather small. Unlike a carrier or freight forwarder, you will not need a warehouse or loading dock. Your clients are not expected to come to your location, so you do not have to worry about a striking reception area or sophisticated offices. In fact, although there are certain advantages to a commercial location, a freight brokerage is a perfect business to start and run from home.
- The place you operate from varies with your resources and objectives of your company. Numerous brokers start from home with the aim of moving into commercial area as soon as they are established with a few clients, which is an excellent strategy.
- The major advantage of starting a home-based business is the fact that it drastically reduces the amount of startup and initial operating capital you will need. However apart from cash there are other things you should consider before deciding on whether you should work from home.

- You should consider the space you will work from, if you have an office where you can set up your equipment and you can work privately without interference. You should also consider if you are going to hire staff or you will be doing everything by yourself. If you want to hire staff working from home might not be practical because you do not want your business to interfere your home functions.
- In contrast, starting in a commercial location needs more capital than starting from home. If you decide to use a commercial location, your range of options will be fairly broad, and your selection should be guided mainly by the goals that you have set for your business in terms of market and growth. Consider office buildings, light industrial parks and executive suites.
- After working from home for several months I found out that unless your home is very large, you will find that a commercial location allows you to create a setup that is more efficient and practical than what you might be able to do in a home office or a spare room.
- It takes a lot discipline, motivation, and focus to work from home. It is also very satisfying to manage your own time and revenue. Sometimes you will find yourself desiring to watch television, do some gardening, do chores, etc. however you must treat it as a regular 9-5 job. My advice would be to get up, take a shower, drink coffee, set a certain schedule and follow it as if you were leaving home to go to work.
- You need to spend majority of the day searching for new customers if you want to be successful. Brokering one load will consume not more than 30 minutes of your time. That includes paperwork, looking for a carrier, etc. As a broker you can earn anywhere from as low as $0 to as much as $200,000 a year or even more. In freight brokerage, just like in any other business, the more you work the higher your returns will be. Realistically, a single person working as an independent agent can possibly broker 10 loads a day and that will keep you plenty busy. But it is good to always be looking for new business.
- Here are some tips that will make working from home easier.

Schedule a work day

- Make sure you set for yourself certain working hours. Even though you are working at home you should respect your working hours and make sure that you adhere to them. If you allow slacking it will interfere with your working hours. Act as if you are leaving the house and going to an office. I would highly recommend getting an office outside the house when it is affordable.

Sticking to it

- Remember that times will be tough. You will need a support system to help keep you motivated. Starting out is the hardest part. Once you have built a book of business, you will find that you stay more inspired.

Avoid Distractions

- I would highly recommend you to have a separate home and work telephone line. Turn the home phone off during the day or you can keep it away from the home office. This will help you in eliminating possible interruptions. You should let your friends and family know that they also need to respect your space and work. Family tends to ignore the fact that you are working and expect you do the things you would do on your day off.

Don't settle for low pay, make more

- Many brokers start by making up to $5000 a month working from home and they settle. They think that they are making more than their previous job and getting to work from home. This exact thing happened to me when I found my first freight broker job, I started making $55000 a year and thought hey I am doing great, I am making almost double of what I was making at Burger King, but after a few short months I realized I wrong I was. The potential is unlimited in this field and you should not limit yourself. You should keep searching for new customers and more freight and more repeat customers you get more money you make. Once you realize it is not hard, the process becomes more like a "rinse and repeat".

Separate family time from work time

- As a broker you will always be on call when you have loads out. At that time it is crucial to separate your work life and your family life. You will find yourself staying on the computer until very late at night trying to contact new customers. You should set the time that you should start working and also the time you stop.

FINANCING

- Having good banking relationships is crucial for brokers. It is not unusual for a new broker to need a line of credit in the range of $250,000 to $300,000. This money will help you to pay carriers before shippers pay for your services. You need to pay the carriers promptly for them to haul your cargo. Therefore other than getting your insurance and license, setting up a good relationship with your banker should be at the top of your list of priorities.
- It is impractical to walk into a bank that you have never done business with, empty handed to ask for a major line of credit. Approaching a bank that knows you will help. You should also have an outstanding credit record because generally a freight broker usually does not have assets that the bank can go after when you fail to pay back your loan. Go to them with a good business plan to ensure that they listen to you.

MARKETING AND RESOURCES

KEEP THESE QUESTIONS IN mind as you prepare your marketing plan:

- Who are your potential customers?
- Where are they located?
- How do they currently transport freight?
- Can you offer them anything they aren't getting now?
- How can you persuade them to do business with you?
- Exactly what services do you offer?
- How do you compare with your competitors?
- What kind of image do you want to project?
- How many of them are there?
- Carriers can be found in directories and trucking magazines. Word-of-mouth is also a brilliant way to locate carriers; therefore when you are out there networking, pay attention to what people are saying about certain trucking companies, and follow up on the ones that have good reports.
- You can also find trucks at truck stops and on the road. Remember that first impressions say a lot therefore, look for trucks that are clean and well maintained, speak to the driver and find out something about the company. If speaking to the driver is not possible, make a note of the company name and headquarters location (it will be posted on the truck or the cab), and give the company a call.
- You will want to treat the carrier as good as your customer. They talk with other carriers on everyday about who they are shipping for and how good/bad the pay might be. They will

also discuss how they are treated. So if you have a carrier that you treat like they were your own family, they are going to tell other carriers.

- Advertising is almost unnecessary in freight brokering. Most shippers are not looking at advertisements for broker that will help them out. You will need to seek out those clients.
- Advertising online or in papers is a great way to gain agents that will broker under you. You can have agents under you, and under the umbrella of a brokerage house. The prospects of what you can do are infinite. This is your own business and needs to be treated that way.
- I would suggest building a packet or portfolio with your company information for customers. Develop a tri-fold flyer, buy some pocket folders, and put together a packet that you can hand out. This will act as a company agent when you are not in front of a client. They can look at it and learn about you and the services that you offer.
- Everything must move at least part of the way to its final destination by truck. With that in mind, it is safe to say that virtually every company is a possible client for you. However, if you take that attitude, you will have a rough time coming up with a successful, not to mention affordable, marketing plan.

Load boards

- Load boards are especially for freight brokers and motor carriers to share and communicate about available loads and available trucks in an effort to make a match. The only loads you will see on most load boards will be other freight brokers and those will do you little or no good because they are not looking for another broker, they want to connect directly with motor carriers that have equipment ready and willing to haul the load.
- There are many load boards on the Internet today. You have Internet truck stop (truckstop.com), 123loadboard.com, getloaded.com, DAT partners, and many more. All you have to do is search the Internet for freight load boards.
  I personally recommend truckstop.com and getloaded.com. DAT has useful tools but is very expensive. If it is provided

by the brokerage you sign on with that is fine. Truckstop.com has carrier profiles that allow you to check a carrier's credit and performance history, forums that you can chat with other industry professionals, and other useful tools.

There is also a free load board out there. Trulos.com is a decent load board that allows posting and searching free to everyone. New sites like posteverywhere.com are available as a service that will take your load information and post it on all load boards.

An example of a load board from direct freight services:

HOW TO CHOOSE A TARGET MARKET

- There are many legitimate reasons for choosing a well-defined slot in the market. When you target a specific market segment, you can modify your service package and marketing strategy to meet that segment's needs. You will also develop a name for expertise that attracts new customers.
- Your target market can be based on geography such as the location of the shippers or the destination of the freight; the type of shipment whether it is agricultural, perishable, oversized, or bulk commodities, the size of loads, particular industries or any other particular shipping need.
- When choosing a target market, you should first consider what types of shipments and shippers you would like to work with. You may choose to basically handle general commodity freight-materials that are not only easy to handle but they don't also require any special attention. You may also choose to develop some experience in areas such as heavy equipment, oversized loads, perishable commodities or even hazardous materials.
- Try not to specialize in commonly accepted fields; instead, find your own niche. For example shipping produce from farmers to packaging companies and then forming a relationship with the packaging companies to ship finished products to the distributors.
- Next you should do market research to determine what the market you choose is like and whether your business will be

viable in that kind of market. If it is, then go ahead with your marketing plan and if it is not, then consider how you can adjust your target market into one that generates adequate revenue.

- There are a lot of carriers operating in the world. Your job as a broker is to recognize the carriers that offer your customers what they need and to confirm their reliability before you hire them.

OPERATIONS

- The principle notion of freight brokering is quite basic: the consignor calls you with a load. You finish your own internal paperwork and then you will check with your carriers to determine who has a vehicle that is readily available. In case you already have an existing relationship with a carrier, you will then fax them an add-on to your basic contract that gives details of this specific load and the charges.
- If the carrier agrees to your terms, the company's agent signs the document and faxes it back to you. If you do not have a relationship with the carrier, you will need to set up a carrier/broker agreement before you conclude the deal on the first consignment. Below is an example of a carrier/broker agreement.

CONTRACT CARRIER - BROKER AGREEMENT

This Agreement made this ___/___/ 20___ by and between
_____ hereinafter referred to as CARRIER and
_____ , hereinafter referred to as BROKER.

WITNESSETH

WHEREAS, Carrier is duly authorized by the Federal Highway Administration to engage In operations In interstate and foreign commerce as a Contract Carrier, by motor vehicle, over irregular routes, in License No MC- _____ desires to participate In the transportation of such freight as is tendered to Carrier by Broker, and

BROKER is a duly licensed Motor Carrier Broker, licensed to arrange for the transportation of property by license ████████████ and controls the transportation of the commodities to be tendered to CARRIER, not therefore agree as follows:

1. BROKER agrees to offer shipment and CARRIER agrees to transport by motor vehicle from and to such points between which service may be required such quantities of authorized commodities as the BROKER may require, subject to the availability of suitable equipment.

2. BROKER agrees to tender to CARRIER for shipment a multiple quantity of loads per year for each year this Agreement remains in effect.

3. SUCH transportation to be accomplished in accordance with the rates and charges and other provisions as set forth in the Broker's "confirmation of contract carrier verbal rate agreement".

4. CARRIER authorizes Freight Broker to invoice Shipper, receiver, consignor or consignee for freight charges as agent for and on behalf of carrier. Payment of the freight charges to Freight Broker shall relieve Shipper, receiver, consignor or consignee of any liability to the Carrier for non-payment of charges.

5. RATES may be established or amended verbally in order to meet specific shipping schedules as mutually agreed, and must be supported by a new "confirmation of contract carrier verbal rate agreement".

6. CARRIER shall maintain public liability, property damage and cargo insurance at all times, with at least the minimum coverage of $100,000 cargo insurance and $750,000 combined single limit liability and property damage insurance per incident on each vehicle. CARRIER will provide BROKER with a certificate of insurance carrier reflecting the required coverage and naming the BROKER as an additional Insured.

7. CARGO shall be picked up at point(s) of origin and delivered at point(s) of destination and delivery shall be made by CARRIER as specified in the Bill of Lading or other shipping documents, which shall be picked up with the cargo transported and shall be completed upon delivery at point of destination to reflect the fact of deliver. CARRIER shall provide a completed Bill of Lading to BROKER accompanying the

freight bill. Each Bill of Lading and freight bill shall contain the dispatch number assigned to each shipment by BROKER at time of dispatch. Any paperwork not sent in to BROKER within a 6-month period of delivery will no longer be considered for payment. BROKER will make CARRIER settlements in net 30 days from point when BROKER receives original paperwork.

8. ALL of the rules as to filing of claims and setting of claims, and all the requirements as to public liability and property damage insurance and cargo insurance that pertain to the CARRIER as a common carrier, shall be equally applicable to the CARRIER on shipments moving under this Agreement.

9. CARRIER shall be liable for loss or damage to any property transported under this Agreement. Such liability shall begin at the time cargo is loaded upon CARRIERS equipment at point of origin and continue until said cargo is delivered to the designated consignee at destination or to any intermediate stop-off party. CARRIER shall promptly handle and attempt, in good faith, to resolve any claims for which claims are submitted either by BROKER or directly by proper claimant for loss or damage to any cargo that is transported by CARRIER.

10. IT is understood and agreed that CARRIER and its employees, sub-haulers, lease drivers and the like are not employees of BROKER. CARRIER will provide adequate Workers Compensation Insurance for its employees in accordance with statutory limits and will have its insurance company maintain a certificate of insurance reflecting the required coverage on file with BROKER at all times. Said certificate shall name BROKER as a certificate holder.

11. CARRIER agrees to defend, indemnify and hold BROKER and BROKER's corporate affiliates and their respective officers and employees harmless from and against all claims, liability and expense for loss or damage to property and/or injury to or death of persons including CARRIER's employees and agents, arising out of, or incident to, or in connection with CARRIER's performance of this contract.

12. CARRIER shall not subcontract or assign any portion of their duties to transport shipments contemplated by this contracted.

13. CARRIER shall file a copy of his ICC permits with broker and will keep such filings current. CARRIER specifically warrants that it's ICC Authority is sufficient to allow CARRIER to transport all shipments accepted from BROKER to its destination.

14. IN the event CARRIER falls to render service satisfactory to BROKER and/or its customers, BROKER reserves the right to hire other truckers necessary to assure prompt and efficient service to its customers. Nothing contained herein shall limit BROKERS right to hire additional carriers from time to time as it sees fit at its sole discretion.

15. THE relationship of the CARRIER to BROKER shall, at all times, be that of an Independent Contractor.

16. CARRIER agrees it will support and protect BROKER's efforts under this contract by refraining from soliciting any customers or shippers of BROKER during the term of this contract and for six (6) months thereafter.

17. Either party may terminate the contract by giving the other 30 days prior written notice of the date of termination. Rights of the parties accrued during the term hereof, shall not be affected by any termination hereof. Any notices given pursuant to this contract shall be deemed to have been received by the other party by the mailing thereof, by Certified Mail, addressed to such party at their principal business address.

18. THIS contract shall remain in effect until canceled by either party from the date hereof and set forth. Either party has the right to end this agreement and cancel or terminate this contract at any time by the thirty -(30) day notice-previously stipulated herein.

IN WITNESS WHEREOF, the parties hereto have executed these presents the day and year first hereinabove written.

ACCEPTED AND AGREED	ACCEPTED AND AGREED
BROKER CARRIER	CARRIER

BY:
_____   BY:_____

_____

TITLE: _____   TITLE:

_____

DATE: _____   DATE:

_____

- After all that, the carrier dispatches the driver. It's a good idea to require that the driver call you to confirm that the load has been picked up and again when it's been delivered.
- After the shipment has been delivered, the carrier will send you an invoice and the original bill of lading. You invoice your customer (the shipper), pay the trucker and then, ideally, do the whole thing again with another shipment.

HOW TO CHOOSE A CARRIER

CHOOSING CARRIERS CAN BE an overwhelming task, especially with so many carriers out there wooing your business. Here are 10 tips to help you keep a clear head when choosing carriers.

Capacity is absolutely crucial.

- Make sure that your carriers have sufficient capacity to serve all your transportation needs. You depend on your carriers to move consignments to their destination claim free without any hitch and in a timely manner. For you to accomplish this, carriers should have the equipment and manpower that is required to meet this objective in every lane they operate for you.

Check financial stability.

- When choosing carriers you are selecting valued business partners who will work with you toward a common objective. Choose a carrier who is going to be a practical partner. You want to make sure that your carrier is financially stable and not in the brink of bankruptcy. The carrier should be willing to reinvest the business and maintain the type of quality equipment necessary to service your needs.

Get references.

- Always look for businesses that are like your own and that will serve as reference accounts for the carrier. You should check the carrier's quality service metrics. This includes performance criteria such as on-time delivery record and damage-free delivery record.

Technology investments

- Your carrier should provide real-time visibility of shipment status and should give you advance warning of service failure that will allow you to respond to your customers. If possible your carrier should have a centralized customer service center, it should have the tools necessary to quickly communicate your needs and/or problems to the proper location?

If you require EDI (electronic data interchange)

- It is needed for load tendering, shipment status, delivery notification, billing and/or remittance; make sure your carrier can support those needs.

Look for excellent billing control.

- It is important that the carriers you select have quality billing processes because billing errors will cost you dearly. Furthermore, make sure that the carriers will be able to provide you with the supporting documentation you require.

Flexibility is a must.

- The carrier you select should be able to handle special requests that you may have. If the equipment that you require changes, the carriers should be able to handle it. The carriers should also be able to deal with and accommodate your clients

Check their service area.

- Ensure that the carriers you select provide service to the areas that you ship to. If it is an interline service, you will want to scrutinize the interline carriers used to service these points just as you would your core carriers.

Look for cooperative solutions.

- Make sure that your carriers share a common commitment to resolving your shipping problems and are willing to find joint solutions to these problems. Furthermore, your core carriers should be partners that will work with you to improve your own operation and reduce costs wherever possible. The issues that they are willing to address with you could cover a broad range of topics, including on-time pickup and delivery service, packaging issues, and appointments.

Don't just shop price.

- Don't fall into the trick of believing the lowest-cost transporter offers the best value. You will discover the best value by considering a mixture of price and service quality. Consider the lowest landed cost, which includes extra charges for expected damage, reconciliation, and invoicing errors.
- The truck capacity shortages shippers experienced last fall are sure to continue as the year goes on. But armed with a good freight broker, you can weather the storm. Many shippers turn to brokers when freight demand far outstrips carrier capacity. Shippers using a broker can access increased capacity without the hassle of managing new carrier relationships.

A quality broker may be the most versatile component in your arsenal of freight service vendors.

How to choose a carrier

TYPES OF FREIGHT

- The different types of freight you can broker are almost endless. The most common are Flatbed freight, refrigerated freight (reefer), van freight, and auto hauling. Other types are; oversized (wide load, extended, maxi, step deck, double drop, Less than truck load or LTL, and more), boats, household goods, government, logs/timber, and the list goes on.
- Your refrigerated freight usually consists of food products, produce, or temperature sensitive material. Dry Vanloads can range from food products to most any material. Flatbeds usually haul metals, large equipment, and other goods that will not fit in an enclosed trailer.
- When it comes to specialized freights, this can be boat hauling, car hauling, extended flatbeds, and more. The specialized market is a good one to get in to. It pays well and is not as flooded as the other freight types.
- You also have your freight forwarding freight types. They are freight that is shipped on container boats, rail, or air. It can be any of the goods you would see in the above lists, just destined for another country.
- Whichever fields you decide to get into, I recommend you do research and make inquiries on that topic. I would say that the simplest, but also most competitive is van freight.
- Your van freight can consist of auto parts, dry foods, papers, plastics and more. It is the least likely to give you any problems during the transport process. When dealing with refrigerated freight, you have to worry about temperature control. Flatbed

freight, you have to worry about straps, chains, tarps, and more. Once you get into specialized such as oversized, boats, maxi, etc.; you have to worry about permits, escorts, and more.

Record-Keeping Requirements

- The Code of Federal Regulations is very specific about what types of records that you as a freight broker must maintain. While you may keep a master list of shippers and carriers to avoid repeating the information, you're required to keep a record of each transaction. That record must show:
  i)   The name and address of the consignor (shipper);
  ii) The name, address and registration number of the originating motor carrier;
  iii) The bill of lading or freight bill number;
- There isn't a specific bill of lading required by federal regulation. Carriers, not shippers or brokers, are needed to issue the receipt or bill of lading, but all that is needed of its content is that the consignor and consignee be named, the origins and destinations identified, the number of packages, the description of the freight, and the weight, volume or measurement for rating purposes be included: 49 C.F.R. 373.
- Customarily, the industry used the uniform straight domestic bill of lading printed by the National Motor Freight Classification (NMFC). This bill of lading traditionally traced the mandatory bill used by railroads and barge lines.
- With deregulation, special interest groups have promulgated a number of different bills of lading. NMFC summoned a group of interested carriers and shippers simplifying its straight bill of lading, to give effect to the changes in recent deregulation.
- It is the company's position that there should be an industry standard and that the standard bill of lading published by National Motor Freight echoes the traditional and acknowledged rules of commerce. It is suggested that motor carriers pay the subscription dues to NMFC (the bill of lading is copyrighted but is not enforced).
- Carriers should note in their rules circulars and contracts that the terms and conditions of the uniform straight bill of lading

shall apply, and that drivers sign non-conforming bills of lading as receipt of the goods only.

i)   The amount of compensation received by the broker for the brokerage service performed and the name of the payer;

iv) A description of any non-brokerage service performed in connection with each shipment or other activity, the amount of compensation received for the service, and the name of the payer.

ii) The amount of any freight charges collected by the broker and the date of payment to the carrier.

o   You must keep these records for a period of three years, and each party to a particular transaction has a right to review the records relating to that transaction.

o   A set up packet for a brokerage is going to contain a cover letter, your credit references, your W-9, insurance, MC number/authority. A carrier set up packet will contain all of the same but include a broker carrier contract. A customer set up packet will include all of the same plus an individual contract that is worked out between you and the customer.

o   All of your customers will need to have a credit limit. If you work for a Brokerage, they will have your customer fill out a credit app to make sure they pay their bills. This is so they don't accept loads from the customer, and never get payment.

Types of freight

EUKOR Car Carriers Inc.

BILL OF LADING

B/L No.
EUKOGBKY1000861

REF DAVID

IN ACCEPTING THIS BILL OF LADING, the shipper, owner and consignee of the goods, and the holder of this Bill of Lading expressly accepts and agree to all its stipulations, exceptions and conditions, whether written, stamped or printed, as fully as if signed by such shipper, owner, consignee, and/or holder. No agent is authorized to waive any of the provisions of the within clauses.

IN WITNESS WHEREOF, the carrier or the agent of the said carrier has signed the number of original Bill(s) of Lading, stated below, all of this tenor and date, ONE of which being accomplished, the others to be nil and void.

Notify Party (complete name and address)
SAME AS CONSIGNEE

ORIGINAL

PARTICULARS FURNISHED BY SHIPPER

Marks and Numbers	No of Kind of packages	Description of Goods	Gross Weight	Measurement
			1,360 KGS	12.096 CBM

1 X USED MERCEDES C200 KOMP ELEGANCE AUTO
REG: AP02 NTC / CHASSIS: WDC2030452R048287
COLOUR: BLUE/SILVER

IN TRANSIT TO BURUNDI AT CONSIGNEES RISK/EXPENSE
VESSEL NOT RESPONSIBLE FOR ACCESSORIES AND OR
PERSONAL EFFECTS AND/OR LOOSE ITEMS STOWED IN
OR ON VEHICLES
MERCHANT SHALL BE RESPONSIBLE FOR ANY COSTS/CLAIMS
ARISING FROM GOODS NOT COMPLYING WITH KENYA REVENUE
AUTHORITY REGULATIONS
USED VEHICLES (S) AND CONDITION NOT KNOWN AND CARRIER
SHALL NOT BE LIABLE FOR ANY DAMAGES AND/OR SHORTAGES
SHIPPED ON BOARD
FREIGHT PREPAID

SAY : ONE (1) UNIT ONLY

"AS ARRANGED"

Date of Issue		No of Original Bs/L
2012, AUG.04		THREE (3)
LADEN ON BOARD in apparent good order and condition unless otherwise stated		
2012, AUG.04		

BILL OF LADING

REF DAVID

EUKOR Car Carriers Inc.

COPY
NON-NEGOTIABLE

SAME AS CONSIGNEE

PARTICULARS FURNISHED BY SHIPPER

1,360 KGS   12.096 CBM

1 X USED MERCEDES C200 KOMP ELEGANCE AUTO
REG: AP02 NTC / CHASSIS: WDC2030452R049287
COLOUR: BLUE/SILVER

IN TRANSIT TO BURUNDI AT CONSIGNEES RISK/EXPENSE
VESSEL NOT RESPONSIBLE FOR ACCESSORIES AND OR
PERSONAL EFFECTS AND/OR LOOSE ITEMS STOWED IN
OR ON VEHICLES
MERCHANT SHALL BE RESPONSIBLE FOR ANY COSTS/CLAIMS
ARISING FROM GOODS NOT COMPLYING WITH KENYA REVENUE
AUTHORITY REGULATIONS
USED VEHICLES (S) AND CONDITION NOT KNOWN AND CARRIER
SHALL NOT BE LIABLE FOR ANY DAMAGES AND/OR SHORTAGES
SHIPPED ON BOARD
FREIGHT PREPAID

SAY : ONE (1) UNIT ONLY

"AS ARRANGED"

2012,AUG.04   THREE (3)

2012,AUG.04

FREIGHT BROKER SOFTWARE

- All freight brokers should use softwares to maximize efficiency and track shipments.
- If you want to be successful you will need some sort of program to manage your freight brokerage business. That does not mean you need to go out and buy a software program that will cost you thousands of dollars today or ever for that matter. Most of people the people who are successful at launching their freight brokerage realize very early on the value of having an easy to use system for effectively managing their customer's freight, invoicing customers and paying carriers.
- If you are willing and you have the expertise you can design and make your own transportation software. You can also buy ready-made software; the choice is yours depending on what works for you.
- The fact is, freight broker software is way better today than it was when it was introduced to the market. Today there are literally dozens of options for freight brokers to choose from when it comes to choosing a Transportation Management Software (TMS) that can simplify their operations and improve the overall management of their business.
- Most freight brokerage software is intended to allow freight brokers to effortlessly enter loads, source/qualify carriers, dispatch drivers, invoice customers and pay carriers. Like any other software, some companies do this better than others and some charge more than others. My goal is to share with you some of the leading providers in the industry

- Technologically- highlighted web-based trucking software applications are reinforcing the work background of the truck firms and freight brokerage businesses. Efficient trucking solutions are not only monitoring the flow of work but also helping by means of combined services for substantial growth and customer satisfaction.
- Trucking software applications are growing and wide spreading in the industry domain as it offers a wide range of formidable business, managerial and operational level, solutions that can satisfy a distinctive workflow process within the organization. The fully featured solutions of trucking software ensure wide-ranging business impact and advanced functionalities in the operational workflow.
- Trucking software applications offer diverse and clear business benefits including: Connecting Resources, Workflow and people.
- Trucking software applications are a great solution that considerably balances powerful project management, online resources management and fiscal management into one simple but not normal easy to use platform. It practically links company's resources, workflow designs, people and operational activities. With its easy to understand and operate modular approach, it blends together all the varied-functioning departments and their activities such as collecting and distributing carrier information, load data, files, receipts, and invoices. Perfectly, it brings all the activities to a centralized level.

One Source of Complete Info

- Trucking software applications significantly reduces the use of paper-based forms, files, folders and other costly stationary items. It directly eliminates the hidden hurdles in the workflow activities that help in providing high-quality output. It is supposed to be the best place to seek complete reports of the organization. Trucking managers can alter the whole manual system into a powerful database system via trucking software, making it a single and dependable source of information for the organization.

Synthesize File Management

- The software reduces the use of statements, invoices, files, folders, and document in workflow processes. It assists in the smooth administration of the files and other information of the firm.

Fused Services

- Integrate services of trucking software eliminates the need of manual navigation of the day-to-day data entry job. It aims to manage detailed information for instant understanding and circulation. Its integrated services help to collaborate with the other divisions of the firm such as accounting, reporting, dispatching, and other main and vital areas.
- The software helps in administrative and operating processes that often comprise of general business activities and make a shielded database management system. It can assimilate with managers, employees, and drivers to know more about the prevailing business requirements. It offers trucking companies the powerful capability to create their business processes; implementing and executing more business activity models at the same time.
- In simple terms, web-based trucking software is an inexpensive and easy trucking software tool that suits the requirements of small and medium sized firms in carrying out their activities at professionally excellent level. It's specifically designed to help trucking companies in collectively decreasing their operating expenses, achieving organizational goals, satisfying a wide variety of global clients and maximizing profits.

Freight broker software

EXAMPLE OF AN ONLINE FREIGHT SOFTWARE

A**RC FREIGHT SOFTWARE SYSTEM.**

Sales screen shot

- Automatic commission calculations for sales staff
- Commission calculations by flat rate, % of revenue or % of net profit
- Sales reporting tools to track performance
- Posting of Commissions to accounting software
- Multiple salespeople can be entered on orders
- Leads tracking; including status monitoring & notes
- Lead can automatically convert to Bill to, Shipper and Consignee
- Spot quotes & Rate Quotes can automatically convert to rate tables and orders
- Rate Tables can be assigned to multiple customers
- Rating by weight, skids, mileage, truck load or footage
- Multi-Currency including Canada and U.S. conversions
- *Arc Groups*™ Module will filter the database and allow salespeople to view only associated customers, shippers, consignees and loads

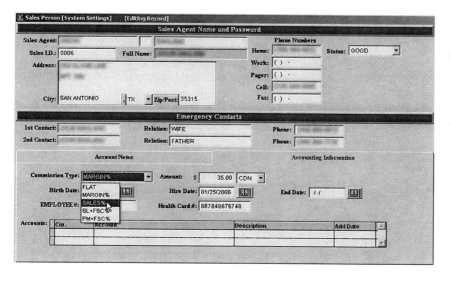

Freight broker software

Dispatch screenshot

- Work Orders (Handles multiple picks and drops, carriers, and custom brokers)
- Comprehensive, easy to search database with shipping histories
- Carrier Searches based on available equipment and preferred lanes
- Carrier Insurance expiry reminders & Request for Insurance Letter
- Carrier Confirmations (Including multiple picks and drops)
- Map & Directions Display
- Load Tracking (color code hot loads. loads picked up, in transit, or delivered)
- Overdue Work Order instant reminder alerts
- Internet Tracking option availability
- Customer Confirmation (created from Work Order)
- Automatic faxing and email capabilities
- Detailed notes stored with each document

Freight broker software

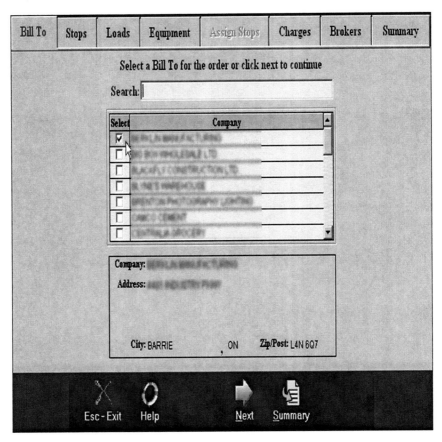

Invoice creation screenshot

- Automatically generate Invoices from Work Orders
- Invoices can be consolidated from multiple Work Orders
- Ability to add extra costs such as fuel surcharge and accessorial charges prior to invoicing clients
- Add additional invoice fees and tax fees that can be calculated manually, by formula or percentage
- EDI option availability

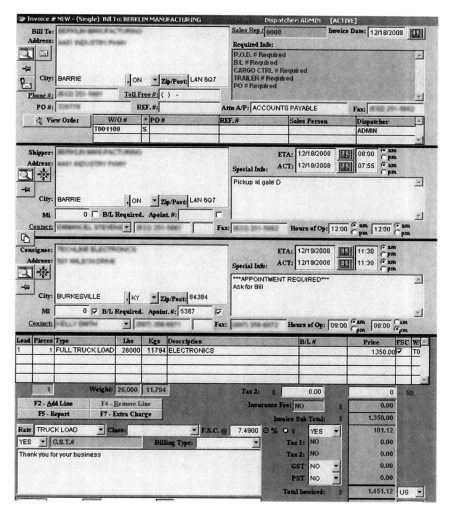

Freight broker software

Report screen shot

- Extensive contact manager (One source database for all information. Simplifies data entry. Easily find Bill To, Shipper, Consignee, Cross-Dock, Carrier, and Custom Broker telephone and fax number, email, addresses, and any attached information)

Freight broker software

- Reports function generates daily, monthly, quarterly or yearly activity reports for sales, operations, accounting, cost and revenue analysis.

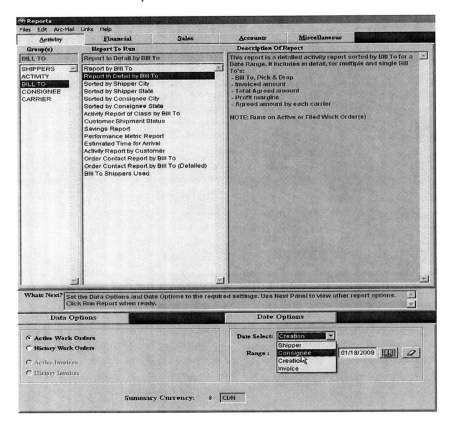

Accounts screen shot

- Exports accounts and Posts Invoices to the accounting package of your choice
- Interfaces currently available are Quick Books ®, Sage 50 ®, Simply Accounting ® and ACCPAC ®
- Other interfaces available upon request
- We can even develop an accounting interface to your customized accounting software

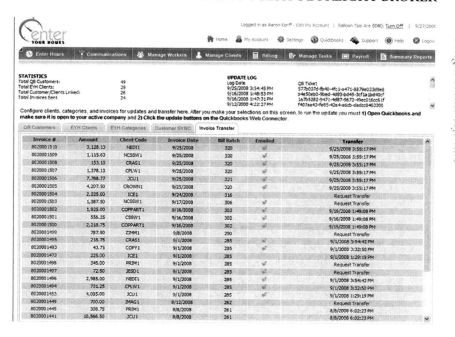

Freight broker software

FREIGHT BROKER INCOME

- Just like any other person working in any other line of work, some brokers are motivated and they stay motivated over the first few months but when they start to see a return, they stop making the calls and stop looking for clients.
- Generally, freight brokers can earn a very good income. There are some who make hundreds of thousands yearly, and there are also a few that make next to nothing. The miracle of this profession is that there is no limit on what a person can make. You are only limited by the quantity of business you can do. Hence, if a person is devoted, hard working, and competent in business as a sales person they can generate much more income than many other professions could provide.
- The average recognized broker makes between $100,000 and $150,000 every year. That is not bad for a profession requiring no college degree, certifications, or state exams. Among start up prospects out there it is also one of the most cost effective. A brokerage requires few costs for start up.
- When a shipper uses a broker, they pay the broker to move the freight, only the broker doesn't actually move the freight, but rather possesses the contacts and resources to find the right motor carrier to do the job. The broker turns around and pays a carrier for a lower price to move the freight than what the shippers paid the broker. This difference is called "spread" and is the broker's profit or margin once operating expenses are paid for.

- So if you charge a shipper $2,000 to move a load, and pay a carrier $1,850, you will retain a margin of $150. Every load will vary, but the current industry average spread per load is probably somewhere around this figure. Load is the most important factor that decides how much a broker makes. How many loads can broker move per week? Most getting started will move around 1-5 loads per week, while established broker might move something like 5-10 or more loads every week. You can see that the annual income as a freight broker will vary directly by the number of loads they move.
- For example, if a broker moves an average of 5 loads per week at $150, it will amount to about $39,000 each year. If a broker moves an average of 10 loads per week at the same margin, they will be making around $78,000 per year. It would continue up from there.

Freight broker income

HOW TO TAKE THE ORDER

- Knowing the right way to take an order is very crucial. Shippers have specific instructions, which they sometimes relay rapidly. You should use a checklist to make sure that nothing is left out. If there is any question at all after getting off the phone, you should never hesitate to call back to get something clarified.
- This is because you have to communicate this information to the motor carrier or his dispatcher and if you have any uncertainty before calling the motor carrier, problems will surely arise. Shippers want brokers are assertive enough to get the proper information and who will keep them fully informed of any potential problems that may arise.
- You should listen very carefully and note the pick-up and delivery instructions, as they are very important as well as any equipment requirements the shipper needs. You should find out if the shipper has made specific appointments for deliveries or whether they want the driver to call in to make their own appointment.
- If there are extra pick-ups or deliveries you need to get a clear understanding of this and then communicate it to the truck. Generally, the truck driver will require extra fees for each extra pick up or delivery.
- If there are unloading fees involved, you need to know up front how much the shipper is willing to pay for it or whether the consignee will be paying for it. Otherwise, you could find profit margin slashed if you end up paying for an "unexpected" unloading fee.

- If shippers are shipping frozen or refrigerated products, they will often ask for a pallet exchange. In this event, they will want the truck to deliver some empty pallets on the pick-up and then retrieve them when the delivery is made.
- Of course the type of product being hauled and the estimated or required weight needs to be noted from the shipper and communicated to the driver. It is illegal for trucks to run overweight and it is up to the driver to control this.
- Last of all, the broker needs to ask for a fuel surcharge. However, if the shipper does not allow for a fuel surcharge, it will be difficult to pay a surcharge to your trucker. Then again, the key is communication and preparation. Find out the details and communicate them to the driver. Make it all happen to the satisfaction of shipper, motor carrier and yourself.

HOW TO BE A GOOD BROKER

Make sure you are licensed.

- Federal law requires anyone arranging transportation for compensation to have a federal property broker license issued by the Federal Motor Carrier Safety Administration (FMCSA). Do not at any time broker loads without your license.

Offer multiple modes

- Most brokers provide truckload motor carrier services only. To make sure you are ahead in the business offer additional service options, such as rail intermodal, airfreight, warehousing, LTL, flatbeds, vans, reefers, padded van, and/or logistics management services. When you have multiple modal options can back up shortages in one mode with capacity in another. This way you will be providing different modes from a single source.

Do a background check on your carriers

- Clients will not trust their freight with any carrier and neither should you as a broker. Before tendering loads to carriers, you should verify the carriers' operating authority, safety rating, and insurance coverage. In addition, a written contract between you and the carrier is essential.

Evaluate your carrier management process.

- To avoid unwanted surprises and problems, brokers must communicate constantly with carriers. Giving instructions over the phone is not enough; a good broker should communicate in writing as well when instructing carriers.
- Explain to your clients how you match carriers to available loads. Confirm that loads are picked up and delivered as promised. Keep copies of your correspondence with carriers and show them to your customers when they ask for it.

Maintain a good credit background

- Freight brokers should be financially solvent and able to pay their carriers. Pay your vendors on time and stay away from legal issues. Make sure that you are financially sound at all times.

Get adequate insurance

- As a broker you will need to carry contingent cargo insurance to pay shipper loss or damage claims if the carrier and its insurance company refuse to pay. Contingent cargo coverage provides shippers a second level of protection, as long as a claim is valid. This will make your customers have more faith in you handling their freight.

Enroll in integrity programs

- Licensed property brokers who belong to the industry trade group Transportation Intermediaries Association (TIA) are required to abide by a strict code of ethics when dealing with shippers and carriers. Shippers will always look for a broker who is publicly committed to integrity in order to avoid problems.

HOW TO RATE FREIGHT

- Freight charges are based on a number of variables, however the two main factors are the weight of the load and the distance it must travel. Rates are also affected by the type of truck needed, whether the driver needs to make one or more stops to pick up the freight, and whether the driver needs to make more than one stop to deliver the goods. Each shipment is entitled to one pickup and one delivery with no extra charge; you can usually negotiate the rate for additional stops with the carrier.
- Before you begin shopping for rates for specific shipments, get an idea of the current "going rates" for the types of shipments you're likely to be handling. You can do this by requesting copies of tariffs from several carriers and studying them
- The commissions you earn on each load generate your income. You will be paid one of two ways:
  i)   You can bill the shipper the amount you're going to pay the carrier plus the amount of your commission,
  ii) The carrier can bill the shipper directly and then pay you a commission from its revenue.
- The most common way to handle billing and commissions is to have the carrier bill you and then you bill your customers.
- Your commission is negotiable, and you can get whatever the traffic will bear. The average broker's commission is between 5 and 11 percent of the shipping charges, sometimes higher. Keep in mind that your commission is your gross revenue, and out of that you must pay your overhead: taxes, payroll, rent, sales commissions, utilities, debts and so on.

- The cost which a shipper (the consumer or business providing goods for shipment) or consignee (the person or company to whom commodities are shipped) is charged for the transportation of goods is determined by a number of factors. The main factors in determining the freight rate are: mode of transportation, weight, size, distance, points of pickup and delivery, and the actual goods being shipped.
- All of these factors play their own independent role in determining the price or rate at which the freight will be transported but they are also all interconnected. When determining which mode of transportation will be used to deliver the freight to its destination there are many things which need to be taken into consideration which will all have an effect on the freight rate. Federal, State, and Local authorities all have their own laws and regulations with regards to the size, weight, and type of freight, which can be transported on their roads.
- Transportation of freight by Rail, Water, or air craft all have their own regulations which take into account Federal, State, and Local regulations as well as safety concerns which contribute to the rate at which freight is transported.
- In general, the more freight you transport, the cheaper it is. This is an important factor in the rate charged to people or companies shipping freight. There are many businesses out there whose sole purpose is to make the transportation of freight cheaper and easier for small businesses and individuals who need to move freight.

How to Build a Customer Base

- Where to start finding the freight is the most important part of being a broker. The Internet will be your most powerful tool. There are websites that list manufacturers. Thomesnet.com is a great tool for contacting shippers. It allows you to email 30 companies a day per account. It is free to set up an account with thomasnet.com. You can email or call these companies. It lists any type of manufacturer from food to metals.
- Another great way is to look through the products at your home or work. See who they are made by, then find them on

the Internet. You will always want to contact the shipping or transportation department and you do find these companies, you need a game plan.

- The industry has evolved from what it used to be. Visiting the business in person and landing an account gained customers. This still happens but in a lower number of instances. It is wise to still do this especially to keep the customer and build a relationship.
- Most shipping departments are now run by a generation that was raised using the Internet. This means that, more accounts are landed through the Internet and email.
- Eventually you will get their email address. I find it easier to land an account with an email. They are usually pretty busy and will answer an email before answering a voicemail.
- Another trick is handling the gatekeepers. The gatekeeper is like a receptionist. They can spot a sales call a mile away and will automatically forward you to voicemail.

How to Build a Carrier Base

- There are many ways for you to find a carrier to cover your load. The first would be to use load boards after you have posted a load. Some may call you off of your load or you can search and call them.
- Another would be to establish relationships with carriers that will haul for you on a regular basis.
- I suggest creating a good relationship with every carrier you use. They will follow you as a broker even if you change companies. And, as you get familiar with your tracks, you can call on your list of carriers that meet the criteria. They will also help you in an anxious situation. If you take care of them, and you are one day stuck with a load, you will find that most carriers will help you and take a lower rate than normal.
- Keep all of your carrier contact information in a software program or an excel file. You will find it useful when you sign up with a brokerage. Instead of waiting to set them up when you use them, you can have your brokerage go ahead and set them up ahead of time.

SELLING FREIGHT TO A CARRIER

- When a customer gives you freight, you have to find a carrier to haul it. This is the easy part. First, make sure you can cover the load. If you bid it too low and cannot find a carrier to haul it that cheap, you will have to give it back to your customer. If that happens, they will usually drop you unless you have been with them a while.
- Once you take the load, you want to post it on load boards. Once posted with the important information (weight, where it picks up, where it drops, miles, your contact info, and type of trailer needed). It is better not to post the rate that you are paying. That might eliminate the chance for negotiation. You can also search for the trucks and call them.
- Once you have a truck interested, you always want to ask them what they will do for the load. You do not have to be the one quoting the price. Sometimes you will need to be tough and firm. This is a part of good negotiations. You should first quote a low figure and let them negotiate for a figure that is just right.
- If you cannot meet them at a reasonable rate, go to the next carrier. Once you do meet at a rate, then you will start the paperwork mentioned above.
- Remember to be fair when negotiating a deal with the carrier. If you quote too low you might cause bad blood between you and the carriers and you will have no one to bail you out when you are in need.

LEGAL MATTERS

- Since freight brokers have to answer for shipments that cross state lines, federal authorities will oversee your business, particularly the Federal Motor Carrier Safety Administration under the 49 CFR §371 rule.
- You already know the basic requirements for freight brokers; an operating license from the FMCSA, the services of process agents, and a surety bond for possible financial liabilities. Here's a quick summary of the other rules that govern freight brokering:

1. Working with Authorized Motor Carriers

- A property or freight broker is part of the transportation business so they go below the oversight of the Department of Transportation. Since you will be working closely with motor carriers (or truckers), you will have to register with the DOT using your FMCSA freight broker license.
- Make sure that you only work with acknowledged entities to avoid risk or liability. That is, the motor carrier moving your cargo must carry an authority that matches yours. For example, if you have a property broker license, then you can only transact loads with a carrier that has a valid property motor carrier authority.
- If you organize a load with a carrier that does not have the right license, say a household goods motor carrier authority against your property broker license, the FMCSA may subject

you to penalties and fines. Frequent violations may lead to a cancellation of your freight brokering license altogether.

2. Record-Keeping

- Both your shippers and carriers have legal access to those transaction records that pertain to brokering services you did with or for them, up to a period of 3 years. After the third year, you can destroy these records.

3. Freight Broker Accounting

- You may have other businesses alongside your freight brokerage. When it comes to revenues and expenses, the law requires separate financial records for your brokering firm. In case your businesses share common expenses - say rental and utilities - third parties must be able to identify what outlays are from the brokerage and what are not. Of course, it goes without saying that you must be able to explain how and why you assigned these amounts to the brokerage in an audit.

4. Misrepresentation

- Whatever advertising you do - whether in print, radio or web - your business must be what you say it is. That is, you cannot go around introducing yourself as a carrier to your customers if you are not. You have to use the same name, which was approved in your freight broker license in any transaction that you do. Misleading information on your broker status can be a cause for liabilities or heavier penalties.

5. Double Brokering and Co-Brokering

- Due diligence is required of all freight brokers, mainly because heavy penalties and liabilities could arise from unethical brokering practices. Two common industry practices - double brokering and co-brokering - present some problems.
- Co-brokering is when you work with another freight brokerage in arranging transportation for a load that you can't handle

anymore. This is legal and acceptable, as long as the agreement with the shipper allows for this arrangement.

- Double brokering, on the other hand, is when a motor carrier contracts another carrier to handle a load you have given the first trucker. This practice is frowned upon and fraught with risks, particularly when shipment problems happen.
- Whether you are aware of the double brokering or not, you may still have to pay the shipper for losses incurred related to the load. Authorities will examine due diligence steps you've taken to determine whether you're answerable for this error or not.

6. Brokering Exempt and Non-Exempt Commodities

- When you arrange transportation for loads from shippers, you must be aware of the following rules governing exempt and non-exempt commodities:
  - 49 U.S.C. 13506(a)(6): list of items that are exempt from USDOT regulation
  - 49 CFR 372.115: list of non-exempt items that are similar to exempt cargo or created from exempt cargo
  - Administrative Ruling No. 133: freight not exempt under 49 U.S.C. 13506(a)(6) as stated in 49 CFR 372.115
  - Administrative Ruling No. 107, March 19, 1958
- You can always arrange shipments that contain unregulated freight. Shipments that have non-exempt cargo bring you under FMCSA oversight. Keep in mind that specific commodities require specific authorities for both freight brokers and motor carriers. The long and short of it:
  i) If a shipment is exempt, then you don't need authority to broker the load nor does it need to be moved by an authorized carrier; and
  ii) If the load is non-exempt, then both you and the carrier need the appropriate authority to handle the cargo.

Failure to comply with exempt/non-exempt guidelines could be grounds for penalties, the suspension of your operating license, or worse, revocation of your freight broker license.

CONCLUSION

FREIGHT BROKERAGE IS LIKE a friend of mine yet just a few years ago I had no idea on what it was. Today I earn around $350,000 per year and I'm very proud of how far I have come. The potential of making money in this business is limitless. The more clients you have the more money you make.

Five years ago, I took a leap of faith and risked losing everything when I quit my job, but I have no regrets. I can now take care of my family comfortably and enjoy my life in full.

Just like a stranger helped me to change my life, I want to help people who are struggling to make a living by introducing them to this business. I would like to motivate you so that you can earn a decent living and enjoy your life.

You do not need a college degree to be successful in this business. All you need a little bit of training, a lot of hard work and determination. If you feel like this is the career for you, then you should visit my website for more information and guidance.

If you like my book, I would highly appreciate it if you give me a good review and visit my blog at *http://freightbrokertrainingguide.com/*. If you register you will receive all future updates and editions of this book for free.

CPSIA information can be obtained at www.ICGtesting.com
Printed in the USA
LVOW10s0244010415

432833LV00003B/228/P